disc

WEATHER WATCH

# Thunder and Lightning

by Alice K. Flanagan

See the light flash across the dark sky. It is lightning! Hear the boom. It is thunder!

Lightning flashes in the night sky.

Lightning looks like a **streak** of light in the sky. It is very bright. But it is only about one inch (2.54 cm) wide.

Lightning is very bright. But it is very thin, too.

Lightning can look like a **jagged** fork that reaches the ground. It can also be just a flash in the clouds.

Lightning can stretch from the clouds to the ground.

Lightning stays in the sky or touches the ground. Around the world, lightning touches the ground about 100 times each second.

Lightning doesn't always touch the ground.

Lightning is a burst of **electricity**. Have you ever had a **shock** after shuffling your feet on some carpet? If so, you have felt electricity. But it was only a very small amount.

Lightning can strike at any time of day or night.

Lightning gives off a lot of heat. The heat causes a loud sound called thunder.

Lightning strikes near a city

Thunder makes many sounds. It can sound like a rumble or a crackling sound. It can sound like a loud clap.

Thunder is loud if lightning is close by.

You see lightning before you hear thunder. Both sound and light travel through the air. But light travels faster. It reaches your eyes before sound reaches your ears.

Lightning can strike bodies of water.

In a thunder and lightning storm, keep away from tall trees and telephone poles. Lightning usually touches these tall things before it travels to the ground.

Lightning moves toward a tree.

Watching lightning and listening to thunder can be fun. But make sure you do it in a safe place!

During a storm, stay indoors.

# Glossary

**electricity (ih-lek-TRISS-uh-tee):** Electricity is a form of energy. Lightning is a burst of electricity.

**jagged (JAG-id):** If something is jagged, it is uneven. Lightning is usually jagged.

**shock (SHOK):** A shock is a spark that you feel when electricity passes through your body. A shock that comes from lightning can be harmful.

**streak (STREEK):** A streak is a long, thin line. Lightning often looks like a streak in the sky.

# To Find Out More

## Books

McTavish, Douglas. *Fried! When Lightning Strikes*. London: A & C Black Publishing, 2009.

Simon, Seymour. *Lightning*. New York: HarperCollins, 2006.

## Web Sites

Visit our Web site for links about thunder and lightning: *childsworld.com/links*

Note to Parents, Teachers, and Librarians: We routinely verify our Web links to make sure they are safe and active sites. So encourage your readers to check them out!

# Index

# About the Author

**Alice K. Flanagan** taught elementary school for ten years. She has been writing for more than twenty years. She has written biographies and books about holidays, careers, animals, and weather.

## On the cover: Three streaks of lightning touch the ground.

Published by The Child's World®
1980 Lookout Drive • Mankato, MN 56003-1705
800-599-READ • www.childsworld.com

ACKNOWLEDGMENTS
The Child's World®: Mary Berendes, Publishing Director
The Design Lab: Design and production
Red Line Editorial: Editorial direction

PHOTO CREDITS: Steven Love/iStockphoto, cover; iStockphoto, cover;
Martha Andrews/iStockphoto, 3; Clint Spencer/iStockphoto, 5, 11; Lyle
Wood/iStockphoto, 7; Paul Schneider/iStockphoto, 9; Luís Fernando
Curci Chavier/iStockphoto, 13; Elizabeth Meloy/iStockphoto, 15; Marios
Theologis/iStockphoto, 17; Marvin Beatty/iStockphoto, 19; Alejandro da
Silva Farias/iStockphoto, 21

Printed in the United States of America in Mankato, Minnesota.
November 2009
F11460

LIBRARY OF CONGRESS CATALOGING-IN-PUBLICATION DATA
Flanagan, Alice K.
  Thunder and lightning / Alice K. Flanagan.
    p. cm. — (Weather watch)
  Includes index.
  ISBN 978-1-60253-365-3 (lib. bd. : alk. paper)
  1. Thunderstorms—Juvenile literature. 2. Thunder—Juvenile literature.
  3. Lightning—Juvenile literature. I. Title. II. Series.
  QC968.2.F56 2010
  551.55'4—dc22                              2009030203